Time Without Number

THE MACMILLAN COMPANY
NEW YORK · CHICAGO
DALLAS · ATLANTA · SAN FRANCISCO
LONDON · MANILA

IN CANADA
BRETT-MACMILLAN LTD.
GALT, ONTARIO

Time Without Number

by

DANIEL BERRIGAN

THE MACMILLAN COMPANY · NEW YORK

1957

Third Printing 1958

Printed in the United States of America

From SPIRIT, A MAGAZINE OF POETRY, published by the Catholic Poetry Society of America: "The Aunt," "The Coat," © 1949; "I Am Renewed," © 1950; "In the Grave Lenten Time," © 1951; "I Sing," © 1952; "Little Hours," © 1953; "The Poet to Himself," "Some Young God," © 1954; "The Innocent Throne," © 1955; "Stars Almost Escape Us," "Pentecost," "Finality," "God Speaks [Said God]," "Loneliness," © 1956, all © by The Catholic Poetry Society of America, Inc.

Grateful acknowledgment is hereby made to THOUGHT for permission to publish "The Moon," "The Men on the Hill," "God Speaks [Said God]," "Credentials," "Believe," "As Rational as Human," "Exaltavit Humiles," "Dream Young Eagles," and "Lightning Struck Here."

Imprimi Potest:

Thomas Henneberry, S.J.

Nihil Obstat:

Martin Healy, S.T.D.

Imprimatur:

✠ Thomas Molloy
Archbishop of Brooklyn
April 15, 1956

Library of Congress catalog card number: 57-10473

to
my mother and father

how lovely
the words never spoken

CONTENTS

Time Without Number

STARS ALMOST ESCAPE US

                    They come unwilling
to greatness, unlike dramatic trees
in chorus, miming man's destiny
with want and plenty, with grinning or tragic
masks.

Size makes no difference. Nor have stars taken
easily to being something other. Their blossoming
momentarily in hedges, depends on a man's
stillness: let him come near, and the doe's eye leaps,
the fireflies leap into a thicket or heaven.

You may decline a whole night of stars
by lighting or snuffing a candle in a closet.
Not one, or all their sum of light taken together,
can keep a stranger's feet on his tricky road.

For what then?
                    the true, the beautiful, struggles
in winds and spaces, and scarcely, perilously wins.

THE CRUCIFIX

(for an eighty-sixth birthday)

I

I remember today a Quebec roadside, the crucifix
raised crude as life among farming people,
its shadow creeping, dawn and twilight, over their lives.
Among wains, haycocks and men it moved like a savior.

So old, so scored by their winters, it had been staked out
perhaps by a band of ruffians on first Good Friday.
The way it endured, time would have bruised his fist in striking it.

What time had done, breaking the bones at knee and wrist,
washing the features blank as quarry stone,
turning the legs to spindles, stealing the eyes

was only to plant forever its one great gesture
deeper in furrow, heave it high above rooftops.

Where time had done his clumsy worst, cracking its heart,
hollowing its breast inexorably,—he opened this Burning-glass
to hold the huge landscape: crops, houses and men, in Its fire.

II

He was irremovably there, nailing down the landscape,
more permanent than any mountain time could bring down
or frost alter face of. He could not be turned aside
from his profound millennial prayer: not by birds
moved wonderfully to song on that cruel bough:
not by sun, standing compassionately at right hand or left.

Let weathers tighten or loosen his nails: he was vowed to stand.
Northstar took rise from his eyes, learned constancy of him.

2

Let cloudburst break like judgment, sending workmen homeward
whipping their teams from field, down the rutted road to barn

still his body took punishment like a mainsail
bearing the heaving world onward to the Father.

And men knew nightlong: in the clear lovely morning he will be
    there,
not to be pulled down from landscape, never from his people's hearts.

THE POET TO HIMSELF

Color it not kind
with skies of love and amber:
make it plain with death
and bitter as remember.

You who set easel
to sigh by willows—
your lie will lie
tomorrow with mildews.

but yours is no shutterblink
transfer of view:
your paint be blood
your canvas, you.

PENTECOST

All their lives rounded in a backcountry brogue
now to see, at crowd's edge, the fine Athenian profiles
agape as bumpkins, scenting their delicate language like
odor of muscatel or honey:

Peter and John, it is Babel crashing about your ears.
The Spirit, impatient of gross and exquisite tongues, of known
and unknown gods, has riven the abominable tower
with His descent. Now the undivided tongues

are abroad, are a wildfire, front the twelve winds from these

transfigured faces. Never again to be constrained
by scarecrow gestures, by hem or haw. Forever to see
agonized at the crowd's edge, the profiles emptied of guile,
their human wisdom consumed in a stench of straw.

THE AUNT

With eyes a dying candle
with voice telling the years awry
my aunt at her high window
counts the seasons by—
bird-wedges or air of snow
or red leaves of a leaning sky.

Eighty-one years have whittled her hands
white coals have whitened her sweet mouth:
Christ has fountained in her eyes
and crumpled her face to drought:
flood and drought, He entered once—
in and never out.

It was all gardens then: young winds
tugging her trees of cloud.
At night His quiet lay on the quiet
all day no bird was loud:
under His word, His word, her body
consented and bowed.

And what is love, or what love does
looks from a knot of face
where marching fires could but leave
ruin and gentleness in place:
snatched her away, and left her Self:
Christ to regard us, Face to face.

THE COAT

This is the coat His bowed mother fitted
at hearthlight weeping fondly. In three seasons—
summer was her angel, fall bent her boughs
a crone winter mothered her maidenhood—
she stitched Him in and out by the nodding fire:
O heartbeat soft as snow on high snow falling,
vein as the veined grape delicate, in and out
my body's shuttle closes you in white linen.

This is the coat my mother's love went buying
to warm me, naked and shivering no one
she heard all night peeking her heart for shelter.
This skin she buttoned to my chin, these eyes
she kissed to light, and gave me over
to the white stinging hand of twelvemonth winter.

It wears me well. She in cunning stole me
from the bolt Christ, won my pattern
wheedling and whispering with Mary at a churchdoor.
I am more kin of Him than hers
who cut and seamed me till her body bled.

O see Him live in me, not I:
I put him on and strut my coat-of-pie.

ITS PERFECT HEART

It was November: an invisible fire
freshened the heart of the grey-blue heron
that had drifted and loved contented
on mild streams, among summer dwellings and children.

But what aroused it powerfully, what call
churned into action its placid domestic wing
that it shook earth like a disease, pettiness and location,
to set breast against wearying and universal air?

Now while dawn streams upward from fields
or early stars send man to fireside
still it labors, aeons above him, by day and night
striding the sunrise, shadowing the red leaning moon

sufficient, remote from the longings of men
as they look aloft: it being vowed to greatness
and powerfully steered by its lodestone, its perfect heart.

THE MOON

This desolate cold god
never created a flower
in his salty furrow,
or called noble birds to climb
and drink at his vein of fire:

he never walked the noon
alight with his own light
whose trees were his sudden fountains
whose waterfalls stood and shouted:

but shod and ribbed in ice
he keeps heart averted
from the plague of youth, from growth:

he has sworn his cold eye
never will heat or approve
the blood that rounds man's breast
and grows the fruit hung there:

poet, mystic, lover
claim his glance for their own:
but only the dead who never
lift eye or cry, or name him
shall own him at the end:

since he and they dwell far
above, below mobbing desire,
and indifferent to each other
separate go their way
into no human day.

CREDENTIALS

I would it were possible to state in so
few words my errand in the world: quite simply
forestalling all inquiry, the oak offers his leaves
largehandedly. And in winter his integral magnificent order
decrees, says solemnly who he is
in the great thrusting limbs that are all finally
one: a return, a permanent riverandsea.

So the rose is its own credential, a certain
unattainable effortless form: wearing its heart
visibly, it gives us heart too: bud, fulness and fall.

JUBILEE

We stepped down fifty years of path: narrow
stile, a wind chiming *cold cold*, and vine
overnight grown old, and kneedeep
in November:
       —stepped to that hearthside, after
fifty years still blooming from fiery stem
with momentary flowers for jubilee.

Dear friends, we touched your withered hands afresh,
your faces: unconvinced how time had ever
harshly or sweetly or at all visited you

more than in a winter garden the winds
a noisy hour strut and orate about.

Turn away, turn to the other's eyes: *absolute*,
absolute grows not in the blind wood
that every day shifts countenance and mood:

not in the garden, eager
heel to heart for summer's hillside run:
but by November breathless and undone.

Your eyes will borrow of the other's eyes
a sun for every lovely or bleak dawn,
gardens will in you live, and a new fire
strike purely from those years of yours
when stars are down.

BIRCHES

Lovely their plumage grew: when winds bore down,
a winged hillside flexed for its flight.

But who moved against these almost disembodied
forms, these scant shadows, hardly more
substantial in full summer than when January
cast them in glass, and shook to ground
for harvest, a thousand shattered bells?

Where they vanished, no angels stood again.
And song was a lost tongue. And the hillside
growing its grass tamely, never again
wonderfully gathered strength to fly away.

EVERYTHING THAT IS

               is not something other:
a ridiculous pablum for the poet's mind
until the wind sing it, or star bring it
ringing its name through the astonished night:

or on a March day, the selfsame crocus struggle
wildly into air, because its roots, through all winter's leveling,
remembered their own name.
                  Or the maple that shook its glory down
puzzle strollers with its identical
and lovely form, four months later assumed again
gradually as a morning.
                  Such things somersault the mind
backward, inward:
                I wonder who knew the stars
from flowers, before flowers were not stars:
before trees spread between one and other, a growth
by night starlike, by day a flowering, and yet itself?

OVER SODDEN ANONYMOUS FIELDS

suddenly from trees that had awaited
in their ragged heights no such visitation—

that voice, out of no predictable country
on the air was there for us: and heart
tired of its wintry beat, crying: *translate!*

But how phrase for the daylaboring pulse
a song outracing all the massive sun,
remaking the world to its own fervent image?

HERE THE STEM RISES

deflowered forever.

the bird is wise only
in ways of quiet

time is a lithe fruit
bending above us

too old for comfort
too raw for falling

here no slim morning
steps out of the sea

no season of snow
no hear-ye of thunder

no chameleon crawling
of youth or of age

not even a now
nor an I nor a you

how many the folded
hands. O how lovely

the words never spoken

IN THE GRAVE LENTEN TIME

when snow wept from the lime
my Love spoke me a little rhyme:

'you whose haste doth weave
a coat of proof against the grave:

'whose love is all a care
for strength of what to wear
on the young breast of fear:

'be not solicitous, love,
for whom to have and have:
I am nailed fast to you: I cannot move.

'nor covet what to wear:
naked as winds O tremble here
till I shall dress you fair.

'love, do not shudder death:
he stopped My word and sewed My breath.
Yet give him gladly: on his day
Love has the final say.

I AM RENEWED

> to rising by that sun
sets courage like a summer round my roots
and welcomes me to stature.

I am renewed to breathing by that bread
sent like a sunrise to my dark
bringing me somehow morrow.

My blood that walks as sullen as a millstream
trumpets the joining of that wine of His.

My life that folds to burial grows bold
and hobbled in its windings climbs the grave.

My ashen words puff up in flame
infused with four winds of a word *arise*.

My hollow breast takes heart at hearing Him
sing like a star above its broken roof.

My feet clear gardens in the greying snow:
my winters die for mention of His name.

O let these words remind His wounds of me

THE MEN ON THE HILL

There is still time to escape
the hill where ruin hangs,
the dry, lax throat of doom.

Tall as veiled spears they hem him,
the proud and diehard women.
Their hearts bleed in their eyes,
their eyes run on to death, their wits
in little feeble rivers run the ground.

Mark what holds them still:—
his spastic dying cry:
for murderers no lightning:
a thirst to curse all springs
our tongues are laid against.

There is less than nothing here.
Nothing were yet something
if stones would rise and grate
a syllable of God: if hands were sprung
a moment only from the trap of nails.

But death has staked him off
and bound him for its baggage:
heaving no miracle, the hill
sighs to a long sun westward:

the sky runs red with torches,
the city blinks us blind
and only death is savior.

THE WORKMEN

This is the body the seasons sold for money—
one by one they guarded and grew his frame:
we were hardly ready for him and he was ready.
This is the one.

These are the nettles sprung from sweating Cain.
Gather them up: they are holier far than flowers:
let us see the brow of the laborer glisten with them.
These are the thorns.

These are the coldiron embers of Lucifer:
these are the arrogant stars pushed out of heaven.
Then give him a handful of stars: heap stars at his feet.
These are the nails.

This is the prime redwood of all the world.
It is tougher and taller than he: it will swing him high:
it will hold him high forever if so we wish.
This is the cross.

I SING

                          the star whose light
my song makes steady,
the face whose look was never
but when my hand had found it,
the word that lovelier stayed
than trees unstressed by season,
what on the earth was seldom
less seldom for my speaking—
pride, delight, deliverance.

This is not greatness, no:
not that consummate gesture
from king whose *fiat fiat*
is blue on distance blue.
His tree-end never dragged
across my coward foothill:
his manacles and thorns
have never clawed or kinged me.

Not these. But few and lonely
the unregarded wait me
to say their *beautiful*
with breath and heart I borrowed:
who but for self I lent
would like me fret and clutter
and be themselves for never.

SOME YOUNG GOD

            had taken this spell on himself
for love of the imperiled. They were sure that in moonlight
he turned agonized features on them; and on storm days

those muscular embattled arms fought all of hell:
but for whose sake, for whom? the children pondered and pondered

whether in full summer they climbed
in and out of him like a father, or lifted their throats
to the enormous midnight clinging his limbs even at noon
or spread hands for the sunlit coins

shaken on them like flowers in high wind, or put curious ear
in a sudden quiet against his breast. One or another,
the youngest, hearing plainly that magnificent heart

imprisoned and uncomplaining, would weary abruptly of play
and sit apart at the great steadfast root, the leather shoon,

thinking: how to release him: what spell would bring him
human, luminous, one of them, into their midst.

It was the kind of dream three summers could fade.

Thirty summers would bring it back: such an ache
at passing, seeing the sawyers hack at the weary god:

that dream, that total childhood, burning at roadside.

OUR VERY HEART

The leaves are fallen, the birds are blown like leaves
from a tall windborne tree that stood at east,
a full and rooted summer, at autumn a full moon
rising. When winter threatened, it shed around
merely an accidental beauty, until the snow
clothed it again one night, a luminous cloud of thought.

But who will measure the height and depth of love
that holds our breath, to hear it now nightlong
wrestle the searching and devouring winds?

By no summer sleight of hand could it achieve
so to arise in the mind, a form of man:
but when death winnowed it, the pure symbol stood
wearing at bone and skull all human affliction
and on that tattered sleeve, our very heart.

MIDWINTER

        and a patchwork snow under inert trees:
yet to their boughs the snowbirds came in a cloud.

It was one to them whether the landscape flowered or withered.
They even preferred this: sending their sweet clamor
into air, they brought to a single tree,

more joyous and numerous than leaves, an entire summer.

Suddenly the tree was alive in dead of morning.
Yet what are these, I thought, to stand against the inhuman
strike and lash of the season? he is the clever fowler
can stalk them from rushes, shake them down
a chaff under his club, what time he would move on them.

But no thought of this. From the living tree they sang and sang.
It was that spurt of courage sends the heart leaping
even in midwinter, into the spring it longs for.

THE BEAUTIFUL RUINED ORCHARD

                    What had November done?
It wore its trees at breast like English swans
on the green swell triumphant and immortal

through spring and summer: so seeing them
from the edge, caught one's breath, to have discovered

perfection in a long single line, dawn to dusk.

But was it threats and mutters of the envious dead
infected, frightened them, that they arose
an immense fleet sailing the autumn storm
fleeing before dawn?
                  Shadow of those wings
fell in blight on the acres, turned their choral surf
to a hoarse whisper through a common sedge.

And where each swan rode like a king to throne: only
a bony ghost the contemptuous wind makes light of.

AS RATIONAL AS HUMAN

Only mid-September: already the doomed
earnest little dancer, the maple, is a cloak of flame.
On tiptoe, here or there, in and out of the pine grove
he mimes and whirls.
                              But the pines ho-hum and yawn
into every wind. They have been there, they will be there
so long, so long, stomping huge feet in the cold,
blinking and disbelieving the miraculous spring sun.

Why then attend or sympathize the doomed
attentive little dancer, shod in cursed slippers,
cloaked in absolute fire, dancing his careful ruinous
geometrics about them?
                              In a few days, the legend goes,
his flame will out: but time will vindicate them
as rational, as human, who welcomed reality with care

a needful distance from its pernicious fires.

EXALTAVIT HUMILES

All things despised, capricious,
evanescent, have an hour of morning. Sumac jostled
by shouldering oaks to the forest edge—how it burns
clearer than they. And cobweb, no more than an afterthought,
trembles at dawn like new-hammered silver.

Someone has overlaid the crouching rocks
with purest lace: they almost stumble to feet
for very pride.
                    The wild brown grasses stand
singing a canticle at the furnace door:
Bless the Lord, rime at morning, frost and cold air!

Even the roots, bound hand and foot, hear and heave mightily,
lie cruciform, and wait the breaking spell.

For a moment nothing is wasted, nothing of no moment:
to the banquet grace calls, grace clothes the unwanted poor.

DREAM YOUNG EAGLES

My poor trees lean on sticks and complain
no matter what the autumn do to ease them.
Can you, seeing them creak their way over field
dream young eagles starting from the orchard grass?

Spring will bear me out. Let them go under,
crotchety profiles of wire, faces the storms hone finely—
they plod and plod their hill, never quite make a shelter,
never are flattened.
                    Give them five months of grace
and see what shapes strike your hillside with furious
beauty: young eagles hardly aground, bounding,
owning the earth: all but crying, all but taking
the whole air with their vigorous mastering wings!

LIGHTNING STRUCK HERE

If stones can dream, after some hundred years
shouldering weight, making a wall inch onward
heaving it up a hill, braking its roll,
being only half above ground, taking the crack

of frost, the infernal sun, the insinuating, sleepy moss:—
if stones can still long to stand up naked, a new creation
with horizon to see what they do, where the wall goes
what shires, forests, it holds—
                              I suppose the dream
might rise, might arc, take color and stance of these
birches that fan out suddenly, bursting the wall
with powerful feet
                      so when we come on them, all that remains
of the neat arranged stones, is a shambles. Lightning struck here
is a first thought. But no: a lovely dream
shook from the mud, the interminable years, and lives.

FINALITY

Trees say in a moment what they have in mind.
Flowers occupy even less time than space.

I once declined the voice of birds: but their import
their flight expunged so quickly, they left behind

only a parabola, an unknown, teasing the mind
out of itself, into their huge direction.

I thought: to diagnose love or beauty is
a cretin's task: to learn not to love
is the slavery.
                    So tree and flower agreed
between blossom and flowerfall: wedded
by the endless ring of the bird's wing, round and round.

So they stand in my heart: one flesh, one perfection.

DUSK

Children at play: I have stood at the single tree
a little apart, to be wound hour by hour into their scene.

The tree at dawn held nothing
in hand, by dusk was faintly clouded
with joy, with thought, with faint commencing leaves.

Had it taken children to its own mysterious
roots, drawn from their roots a palpable growth,
a longing to be a child?
                              I saw it swing
in the light wind, its shadow envy
so longingly all their pirouette about it,—

if one regarded merely shadows, if one were willing
to turn appearance to a truth,—some chance note,
some touch of hand had smote the spell.
                                        One child more
whirled all an innocent afternoon away.

THE INNOCENT THRONE

(for Philip)

I

My laced and living memories arise
suddenly as those boughs our boyhood grew:
challenge and portent.
               Who dares climb
the stallion tree furiously striding heaven,
and ride, ride, beautifully to subdue,
to match, to curb?
                  Or diminished in Sunday twilight
what clean young figure, innocent of blood,
dares with his cape the avalanche, the horn?

My nightmare passes and the sweet day dawns.

But Christ: to what have you brought him? he rides now
the bleeding horn: he hangs from the furious bough.

II

Games were marvelous. To pretend king
set heart nobly on edge, gave the stick of sword
a superb damascan ring. And what more
could ten of the uncertain clock bring, awry,
authoritarian, than neighborhood children crying
hail, all hail: than passage to an innocent throne
and dragon years all slain?
                  Folded the crown in dust
these twenty years: never an inquiry
the old air forms: *wears he still at breast the heart
once, at ten of clock, redressed our wrongs?*

Now all the bells of heaven seize the sweet tale:
the young heart, its pretend, were true: *all hail!*

III

At play on summer's stream, we watched
ourselves, our paper boats, flowering
in underwater light: and stretching a hand
to greet the stranger, found and lost
his shy image forever.

Then a cloud stole its wavering sun away
and downstream the boats limped into evening.
But where had the game fled, the shouts
that scattered waters swifter than white flocks?

A first star knew, that could see for miles
the ins and outs of this most secret water:
where it wore proudly at breast the children's faces
never to change, with no disfiguring tear
and all their songs carefully folded in echo.

IV

Hide and seek, and dangerous twilight
stands with the lurking and lovely brother

who in a corner east of the new moon
is wound in such a spell, suddenly one stops
short of touch or shout. O is it time
that grows his shadow to an angry sky

or takes him suddenly by hair of head
to the immeasurable treetop, or swings him
over a wall no love shall clamber?

Blind, count ten at the wall, and go
afraid and tiptoe under conniving trees:

he is here, he is there—
                              heart, he is nowhere
but age will show him, a sudden flare
lighting the sudden stranger.

V

Now and again, apart in courageous
imagining, we wheeled upon the dark
and dealt with those tremendous cowards
in circle perilous, with a chanting sword.

again, we had merely to step on shore
and first drum of a foot would send
time and his dragon sliding back.

knowledge was not in the mind: was approach
slowly, watch from shelter, capture.
knowledge raised its own device, gave the lie
to appearance, stood on evil slain

or bending over flowers in the hand
heard secret heartbeat: or east of sun
standing, or west of moon, snapped the spells
that had wound men arrogantly in toils

and given bestial forms to beauty.
It was good, turning quietly to slumber
to bid stars be wakeful, to bid one's dreams
create straightway a marvelous morning.

VI

A son's identity can startle
even the mother, upon whose limbs, whose life
this child has clung. He has stepped out of her
as image from its mirror, has danced before her

figures of her own grave and watchful will.
In the secret house of each, the other dwells.
She has walked easily into her child's eyes.

Then on a day, that subdued and smiling pulse
grows brutal, grows tragic, snatches his heart away.
What has befallen? *Thy father and I
have sought thee sorrowing.* A stranger suddenly
stands at her door.
            O has love grown, built up
her lintel to his height, heart to his heart's
new mystery, that she can bid him welcome?

VII

To every day, like a creator you bring dawn.

When our host, our Lord, goes up, up goes the sun
and spirited birds start, and men afield or factory,
and supernatural spring, under glacier ages long
flows again in the underground vein, grows in green song:

in stony and desert soil the tender new flowers
hear His call, raise tendrils to His face:

how He pours all heaven into blind eyes with His look
and the astonished dead stand up with a canticle!

Stand high, Sun, in perpetual noon nailed to our day,
raining nourishment and youth from the axel tree:

to Whom the laborious world may come in any season
and climb, and taste your unimaginable fruit.

SAID GOD

When the word struck, it was all fountains
first. Trees slowly followed, feeding, nesting
their burden, until winds shook
their harvest delicately to the day.
But from this utter reach, this masterful root
the hundredfolds or cockle who shall say?

He is no tide, turning speechless in love
to any face the moon shows. This rational eye,
this hand, follow no dumb vane or weather.
He casts his hunger, his magnanimous heart
down his own road and sea: to hell or to Me.

Nor only a curious living mirror
spinning and seeking in the world,
coaxing the sun to his side, taking
in absolute draughts the whole day to breast.
I shatter the lying mirror for his sake:
he must take Me or break his infinite heart.

Then I name him child: I name myself Father.
My eye upon, within him, sees all ways,
my hand that hung the fruit before him, swung
his heart's pendulum between it and Me.
And I am sweet beyond it. O taste of Me.

I name myself his spouse: I leap
continually to his presence; He lies
closer in My arms than speechless Eve.
And though he breathe and drink her fulness:—
lovelier than love's body, more tender than she
I call unutterably and he comes to Me.

II

I would even give my Son to them.
In a field of flowers, wide as dawn to dusk,
one hesitant flower more, only one more:

or in a sky already great with stars,
one star more at the edge, hardly in evening.

He will not make turmoil: one child more
allowed by his father's hand into a park of children:
one voice adds little: one voice to a sweet choir,
another among the swings, linked in a ring-around.

They take him easily to heart: more is but
merrier: at table, in bed, he asks
so little a corner of heart or world. He will never trouble
the country children of men with who am I.

Only to bend intent over their games: never to say
Children: I am all your bloom and odor and starlight.

III

The thousand and one exchanges of love,
properly and jealously human, I am not stranger to.

Nothing so takes the eye as flowers: nothing so
delicately translates into surrounding air all
the heart cannot bring itself to, flushing and paling

yes and no. But the rose has drawn
wisdom to her being in a great flood: she can speak.

I have contrived too the soft nightfalling air, the hour
striking directly on soul, making tremble its pure

suspended metal.

All these, and more, and Myself, compounded in my sweet Son. O language of love, neither shout nor violation.

But of starlight, light: of flowers, candor: of Myself, my love.

PARABLE

I dreamed: in starved vicious soil
a miraculous seed took root, changing
all evil to its own good uses.

Men who dwelt or labored in that place
did its upward thrust encounter, a two-edged
sword divided or impaled,

a death that day had not provided for:
or swung and hung them, living ornaments
from its boughs. They were dazed

to see that infinitely dear world flee them,
a beast scuttling into its hole of space:
themselves swung upward in a terrifying
careless trundle.
                    One man I heard cry
loudest of all in that desperate mischance:
Christ, this be my hour, and I at last
a soul

HAYDN: THE HORN

Now that compelling silver throat
breathes its own form on the air:

first a green world all renewed,
then with a more knowledgeable and piercing cry

hunter and hunted leaping
tangible, but also into air.

Turn, turn the green vase—
an obbligato raises at the spire
a further angel and his dizzy trump:

or into a roadside mart descends
of children tricked and marched out endlessly
at the pieman's airy heels:—

in and out of mountains
bearded and fresh of face

all the grandfathers step, all the
grandchildren, rubbing their eyes

so purely looking toward
even us

They are filled, vein and throat
with music, they lightly stand

as long as music.
Diminuendo, sweet end of phrase,

all are gone: that impossible
lovely vase they dwelt upon:
gone, gone

IN MEMORIAM (E.M.)

I

No vine on the black hillside has death harvested
cleaner than this holy body we bid farewell.
A word, even the brief apologia *love,* to lighten
this dolorous falling away, were aeons beyond him.

Before that glance again shall spring a season,
God will stand at the sun's throne a thousand years,
and we call and call, and stars fall
in a nightlong rain.

Yet I take courage like a stone instrument in hand
while the tears start, to score his features large
on time's dumb face. It was no abstract death
had its way with him. The white Christ of the altar
broke him apart: that Wine he raised
desired and drank him to its hungry heart.

II

In deep of winter, when no one dared promise
April to his heart, and springtime lay
too many months away for his poor search,
too far for his gesture ever again to dress
tired trees in a new season,—

                the old priest lay dying:
and I at bedside testify—no archangels,
no prophets ever spoke, compassionate or terrible:

                Even the Host
bending to him like a lover, stood beside
at the end unrecognized. It was the last mystery
to trouble him or us. Afterward, his eyes
said in their closing: welcome Archangels: welcome, May.

III

Death that had worn so many masks, tragic and cunning,
and called himself thief, enemy,—came to this place

quiet as a winter sun: no violence, no voice. All the day long
nightlong, we remembered invisible Jerusalem
and the king's temple that went up, stone on stone
with no sound of hammers breaking the holy hours.

And we praised death for his singular courtesy
who had not stolen or murdered our priest at all,

but gave us at evening, when we came fearful
of his dominion, such ivory features and limbs
as weary centuries away in some dim chancel

or What on a mild twilight, by light of the first star
that holy mother received at heart, and was comforted.

LITTLE HOURS

I

Mother, at that word your eloquent body spoke
I search another word vainly as Gabriel.
O witnessing your consent, he saw how love
planted an axis so deep in our human soil
that history, fear, defeat, aeons and nations
turned, would turn forever about your village room
declaring like figures in time's rickety tower
the lightning strike, this only and central hour.

Whom the world could not contain is detained in you.

Since Love in entering, so builds your hidden doorway,
consent again, receive me for child I pray:
your nourishment, your silence, your face averted,
your hands serving excellent bread and meat: your heart
ages apart in its own country, its heaven descended
to four low walls and a dim evening fire.

II

Winter is hard: it reminds us how that mother,
heavy and meek at term, set foot on her dolorous road.
Her trees, all ample and tender at summer
were slit and groaning beggars the wind went through:
the sun that had clothed and companied her angel:
what fierce looks from him, and scant comfort now!

Mother: because the ungracious season should have risen
—at your footfall, for knowledge of whom you carried,—
into such June as shames all deserts to bloom,
leaps cliffs with roses, melts the tigerlike ice
into tame brooks for you—

                                    because northwind still blew
and summer hid cowardly: —enter stilly my heart
whose winter your first footfall breaks all apart.

III

Like a waterfall, from what height falling
he came to her; falling, filling her body.
That vessel, brimming with him, O never shall fail.

or entered her like a sun its morning, starting what flowers—
from her footfall and welcome, an inextinguishable day.
that dawn lifting light to us, O never shall darkness own.

or came in echoes of that living anvil
forming him, calling him: be loud in me, love O loud:
until his thunders owned her breast utterly.

he came as tongue to her bells. O from that shaken
and living tower, what music flies: my soul
does magnify who makes my body great.

or came in a tide, riding her pure lands under—
but tender, O living rain: he fell to her to rise
in hundredfolds up from her secret garden.

But mostly in need, asking her flesh to clothe him.
O because love ran uncontrollably to that meeting,
from her arms, her breast, He walks into our lives.

IV

So when she held him close in the firelight, her adoration
stood round him, came out to him like stars.
Or when between tasks she glimpsed him from the doorway
her being sang, her heart rang out to him:

'From the Father's arms did he call me: O did I run
calling my Ave Ave, summoning that Dayspring?

he was born of me: I am born continually.

when I lead his footsteps in wonderment through his world
naming flowers and birds and trees to him, I read in adoration
always the infinite lucid page: the Father's Word in him.

when he turns his grave eyes in questioning on me,
strikes me like lightning: the Father's Son, my Son.'

V

He too, he too shook vainly as a flower
above the teetering world; he blindly crept
murmuring this way and that, the unsteady hour.

or saw under glass the diamond spring
cracking white light to color: saw the day rise
and the moon fall wonderfully to his eyes.

and the world widen when he touched its wall
and grasses shrink when he stood unsteadily
above them first; how the season fell

crashing its beleagured leaves and trees.
water coiled and examined coolly his hand,
furry white snows nipped at his heel.

Later his sentences struck. First there was time
to set his heart beating painfully to our rhyme.

BIOGRAPHY: CHRIST

Who you are
let astounded midnight say
that saw itself flooded with day

or springtime that came around
subtly on the world's wheel
and saw you, small and larger, walking its ground

or, sweet on a boy's tongue
the suave air making your words
and taking them grandly, a whole summer of birds:

let that mother tell
whose total heaven was small
between hearthside and village well

or the dumb tree that bears
pegged down, posted as ours
forever, the unsearchable human years.

LONELINESS. (Joseph speaks)

To be a part of things, to be apart from them:

Every spring I dunged and pruned the peach row
on south hillside: every autumn, like a stranger
took down the fruit whose face met my surprise
with its odor and wet, only half remembered or deserved.

Or watched from a doorway, artisans
summoning out of a dumb stick some form of beauty,
the fine grain emerging along hand or arm like a pulse,
every sigh of the blade saying, *I did not do that.*

Or parleyed with old trees in my yard
that shift painfully in the noon wind, heads together
nodding a memory awake. I did not lead them there:
they were already old when my father slept
a boy's hour, a drowsy noon in their shade.

I had even less to do with the stars
that having led her to me, bring her still face to me
evening and dawn, making of evening and dawn
one tranquil ecstasy.
                    Blade, hoe, manhood—
what have my tools to do with What wakes in her?

MAGI

They set out in bright approving summer:
flags, gold, imagination attending
down charted roads, the star like a sun of night,
and at earth's end, the unique King awaiting.

Autumn too was lovely and novel: weather temperate
and the star mellowing slowly as a moon.
Then winter on them: the light snuffed out:
hearsay, frontiers, men inimical to dreamers—
and what direction in iron snow?—a hind's track
diminished in ivory, a white birch stricken to ground
and the sky tolling its grey dispassionate bell
upon age, upon infinite heart's weariness.

So the great came, great only in need
to the roof of thatch, the child at knee awaiting.

RESURREXIT

I: Thomas

Of that instantaneous flower he wore for body
nothing, nothing of nature can ever convince us.

Nine months in borning takes root in mind too:
Mary's process is buried in us: but out of what cave
between dusk and day, did ever Flower strike
earth's drumhead before or since, so healing a blow?

Slow, slow to follow him is spring forever
and unfolding children, by many dawns only half
persuaded to flower.
                But this instant soul
stood his straight waiting body under its waterfall,
summoned his flesh to glory in a moment.

Nothing of nature, not even children convince us
save we have seen, save we have breathed those wounds.

II: Never Again to Be Safe

Of course death was hard, hard for the poor.
Yet one's heart finally took it in stride,
closing a father's eyes, seeing the mild slumbering
seas turn monstrous.
              But this:
not even inland trees, in a whole lifetime thrust
could match that easy angelic afterthought:
                      Approachable God
had been so reduced to friend, so mildly poured
over days and years: there were no words left
to meet this hard exchange, this other side of death.

Whether we turned locks on us in a remote alley
or pushed off into seas and stars: the dawn
rose to him, evening breathed him.
                         It was always
never again to be safe, summed up our lives.

III: BELIEVE

That delicate honeycomb Christ took to mouth,
that plundered nest was sweet, to lips grown grey
with Judas kiss and gall. Not since Mary's milk
had ever the earth offered in cup or lip
such word as the shifty bees, this way and that stealing,
assuring: the dead flower lives: even death serves.

The dismembered fish too,
ikthus for Christ, stared up at the fearful
fishermen. They tossed unseaworthy
when the walker of waves stood there, and the floor
pitched them green. When he had eaten away all
but literal arrangement, the skeleton said
Jesus Christ, Son of God, Savior.
                         Death again: the eyes
even of a dead fish crying: believe or drown.

IV: THE UNHURRIED TREE

Christ: because your soul sought its body again
a chance tree reminds me of you: root to top
shaken with its own will—to be itself a sun,
to stand among children and men, a companionable

spring. Women who came to mummy you: no tree,
they should have seen, shook bones in the dawn wind:
but on that road, every one stood in its commencing flesh
and said before the angel with a new tongue

I am risen. A hundred resurrections lined their dawn
but they thought only: we will give his ghost cold comfort
and wind that body like a Pharoah in long linen.
They had nothing to offer life. Of what use in that mouth

honeycomb or fish? He must grow his own flesh
bright again, sweet again, a tree from its own root.
They stand where he cast the squared stone aside
that hindered his giant throat. They run and run, but the news

is all on wing, is far as the tremendous drowning
world of trees, that first drank from his infinite
roots: and now runs far ahead, as far as years
arriving on my morning, with my unhurried tree.

THE CASTLE (Heidelberg)

Even the elegant monuments have stopped breathing,
their buttons and swords dropped, their suave features blank.
Now an icecream day, a sun's snapping lens
make mock of these gentlemen awry, these leaning towers
whom children and time undo, whose shadows flee them:
at length proved wrong, proved dolts and dispensable.

Then in one place, a flush of roses rooted and fed
in dust, climbs armor and ruined lace
regardless: at looted heart
it blooms and beats, a marvelous revenge.

EACH DAY WRITES

                in my heart's core
ineradicably, what it is to be man.

Hours and hours, no sun rises, night sits
kenneled in me: or witless and lovely as spring
a total flowering takes me in an hour
and I tread my own heart amazed: what land,
what skies are these, whose shifting weathers
now shrink my harvest to a stack of bones;
now weigh my life with glory?

                Christ, to whose eyes flew,
whose human heart knew, or furious or slow,
the dark wingbeat of time: your presence give
light to my eyeless mind, reason to my heart's rhyme.

THIS WORD OF GENTLE LINEAGE

has no charge
laid on it: to oppose, convince, elevate
is foreign to its blood, that has run reflective

through arteries of this possibly best world.

Possibly best: actually stubborn, masked,
stillborn: requiring above all a searching
imagination laid to it, a deliberate self-
imposed stillness
so of surf and field, of man and season
a viable encounter be conceived:
corner doorway,
a face in shadow there, a fall of snow,
a storm or star:
the frail admissible clue
ferried by gentle or by vicious tides
to shore, to sea floor. But a permanence.